BOA
EDITIONS
LIMITED

News of Home

*

Poems by
Debra Kang Dean

Debra Kang Dean
October 2001

*

Foreword by
Colette Inez

BOA Editions, Ltd. * Rochester, NY * 1998

LC #: 98–72186
ISBN: 1–880238–66–7 paperback

First Edition
98 99 00 01   7 6 5 4 3 2 1

Publications by BOA Editions, Ltd.—
a not-for-profit corporation under section 501 (c) (3)
of the United States Internal Revenue Code—
are made possible with the assistance of grants from
the Literature Program of the New York State Council on the Arts,
the Literature Program of the National Endowment for the Arts,
the Lannan Foundation, the Sonia Raiziss Giop Charitable Foundation,
as well as from the Mary S. Mulligan Charitable Trust,
the County of Monroe, NY,
and from many individual supporters.

Cover Design: Geri McCormick
Cover Art: "The Leap," by Lynne Feldman, courtesy of the artist
Typesetting: Richard Foerster
Manufacturing: McNaughton & Gunn, Lithographers
BOA Logo: Mirko

BOA Editions, Ltd.
Richard Garth, Chair
A. Poulin, Jr., President & Founder (1976–1996)
260 East Avenue
Rochester, NY 14604

for Brad and David

Turn back to being an Uncarved Block.
—Tao Te Ching

Contents

Foreword by Colette Inez   9

PART ONE: IMMIGRANTS

    Stitches   17
    Inside My House   18
    Aloha, 'Āina   20
    The Hollow   22
    Proteus   23
    Heal-All: In Memory of Kana Nakama   25
    Immigrants   27

PART TWO: THE CORSAGE

    Obake   31
    Marginalia: Honolulu, 1970   32
    Spheres of Influence   33
    With My Mother and Aunts in the Kitchen   34
    Calling from the Gate   35
    New Year's Eve   36
    Back to Back   38
    The Corsage   39
    Courage, Temperance, and Wisdom   41
    Island Fever   43
    In the Way Back   45

PART THREE: HOMING PIDGIN

    Bruises   51
    Smoke   52
    In My Father's House   53
    Pineapples   54

Wild Horse Island   56
Homing Pidgin   58
No *Pilikia*; or, Piece of Cake   59
Hawaiian Time   60
Taproot   62
Syllabus   64

PART FOUR: Catch and Release

Fishing the Sky   69
Becoming One of the Guys   72
Distance   74
Catch and Release   76
World Enough   78
On the Eve of My Thirty-fifth Birthday   80
Prothalamion: Of My Brother in Los Angeles   82
Fidelity   84
Blue Apartments   85
Because I Could Not Go Home for My Aunt's Funeral   87
The Weep Line   89

Notes   91
Acknowledgments   92
About the Author   93

*

Foreword

"My folks," Debra Kang Dean writes to a friend, "have finally forgiven me / for ruining the family reputation." Half Okinawan, half Korean, born and raised in Honolulu, she enlisted in the US Air Force after a semester at the University of Hawai'i at Mānoa and became, as it were, "one of the guys" training at Holloman AFB in New Mexico. Provocative material for any dust jacket.

She now resides with her *haole* (Hawaiian for Caucasian) husband and family in North Carolina, and from the Tarheel State contemplates states of pleasure in the here and now, and what pulls her toward the landscape of the past. Full of heart, yet keenly observant and grown canny in the Big Fifty, Kang Dean has tasted her share of American pie and savors it. "Tell me Hawai'i is not my home / and watch me explode." I don't doubt her for a moment.

A passion for home's recollected terrain takes over in "Stitches," a sonnet in which fragmented time repaired to wholeness preoccupies her: "Nothing fits the contours / of the landscape I was born to—absence / of mountains, dense green, and salt air that smothers / like family, like the waters I breathed penned / in my mother's womb."

Grouped into four sections, her book deals with the immigrant experience, home thoughts, and childhood milestones. Poems of departure from the islands to northwest and southeast mainland actualities round out a bountiful collection.

Whether she is writing sonnets or sestinas, syllabic poems, three-beat lines or rhymed quatrains, the poet offers us insights into family. We meet tough, hard-core smoker Grandma Lee, part of a wave of immigrants "invited" by King Ka-lā-kaua to work the sugar plantations. Grandma speaks almost no English, holding fast to traditions that put her at a remove.

Heeding her Korean ancestry, Kang Dean inspects intolerance in the Aloha State. "Back where I come from / they call my father's people Yobo, kimchee, / the Irish of the East." A feisty identification with prejudice also says something about the poet as prospector, Geiger counter sensing different frequencies. She leans in to detect clicks from ghosts of the past in "Courage, Temperance, and Wisdom," and pens a letter-poem:

> Dear Annette: Sixteen years ago our mothers
> were not much older than we are now.
> God, how we hated their stupidity

and submissiveness and swore we'd not repeat
the pattern of their lives.

Later in the same poem, given the benefit of distance and now mother
to a son, she sings a more reflective tune: "Sometimes / I think this pursuit
of philosophy / is likely to give me only words for things / my mother had
already taught me."

While Kang Dean takes an uncompromising look at her parents, she
understands their predicaments. Writing of her father, she draws on a famous
Zen koan to address the roots of his emotional isolation:

My father's life is the sound of one hand
clapping. Against his body a stepfather
lifted an open hand or fist. His mother
drank hard liquor and smoked unfiltered Camels.
He sealed himself shut like a safe.

In "Back to Back," a savvy poem in rhymed couplets, mother and
daughter compare heights in a test the mother wins by an inch. Tenderly
imagining her as a flamingo poised on one foot at the sink, the daughter offers
to peel potatoes to allay feelings of competition. She shrewdly divines her
mother's silence as coming not from lack of feeling, but "want of words."

Words are important to Kang Dean, who loves their byplay as in "*Aloha,
'Āina*," twelve tightly sprung triads that wittily shuffle time and numbers, and
take a swipe at developers in Hawai'i: "In '59 statehood took the 'i' / from
reality leaving us / only real estate."

She is also enamored with the sounds of language, near and pure
rhymes, the alliteration of Hawaiian compound words, *lomilomi* salmon,
holoholo, and delights in punning cadences that mark out time: "Iamb. Iamb.
I am." She knows "plosives, / / fricatives, glottal stops" are what lips need to
speak of the heart. And as she salutes the stoicism of the working poor, she
is on easy terms with pidgin, obliging us to recognize sharp-edged, melodic,
or guttural lines as they fall on the ear. Listen as down-to-earth courtship
memories rise up in "No *Pilikia*; or, Piece of Cake," an account from an
islander to whom she pays tribute:

I been married for seventeen years.
I met my old lady Ala Moana Beach Park.
I wen' said, Us go have one beer.

T'ree months later she almost bite off my ear.
See da scar? She *huhū*, 'cuz I wen' take
Another *wahine* out. But no *pilikia*.

Possessed of a fine ear for speech and a knack for making apt analogies, she shows us the flair and exactitude of a seasoned writer. As she describes a dull teacher's drone we get the unerring drift of "Her voice—how can I say this / kindly?—was like the hum / of an overworked refrigerator, / constant and keeping things cold."

Family talk in the kitchen, sometimes accompanied by a hot game of *hana*, is rendered with warmth and exuberance. Cloistered with her sisters away from beer drinking men mesmerized by football, an aunt coins nicknames for her niece and teases: "*niele*, Miss Nosy, Miss Big Ears."

"Intellectual" in pidgin converts to "him think big." Transcending gender difference, Debra Kang Dean thinks big, sharing a sense of her life as it arcs from Oʻahu across the Pacific to mainland USA. A poet reconciling words, doing honor to the language, telling us what it means to be alive "free to look in both directions, / behind . . . and ahead," she is a valued resource. With her first book, she makes a memorable and exciting debut. Bravo!

—Colette Inez

*

NEWS OF HOME

PART ONE: Immigrants

Stitches

What can I say? I've even forgotten how
to busy my hands with scraps of needle-
work, dumb hands unwilling to commit to
what the heart won't. Instead, I sit idle
staring out windows. Nothing fits the contours
of the landscape I was born to—absence
of mountains, dense green, and salt air that smothers
like family, like the waters I breathed penned
in my mother's womb. Hard to say when I
chose this· nothing the hand does
can stitch time back to that place where mind and eye
might mend the world to wholeness. Always
two worlds. What pattern governs this surface
inscrutable as the ocean, my mother's face?

*

Inside My House

I remember wishing
that drumming on the table
would stop. I followed
the arm up the elbow,
the shoulder, in search
of a face, so I could tell
whoever it was to stop.

Having reached the shoulder,
I could see no farther.
I stared at the hand
as it drummed on the table.
I thought hard, "Stop!"
It relaxed, then started again.
That hand was my—her hand.

No one believes I've slipped out
of her body. I dreamt it, though,
and told the doctor who readied
the spinal. I feared it. In recovery,
I woke to find it was so—
they told her it's all in my head.
I don't know how

we could live without mirrors
now. The inside of my house
is all mirrors and windowpanes.
After I've watched her eat her breakfast,
I can turn from the mirrored walls
and, through the nearest window,
count cars and people as they pass.

When I tire of that, I turn
back to the mirror where
out of its glass, she stares back.
If I should turn from the mirror
for even the briefest second
as she begins to stand,
she'd slump to the floor.

In mirrors I watch her walk
up the stairs and through
the hallway—left foot, right.
I concentrate so hard on her feet
I can't see what she's looking at.
She plops down at the foot of the bed
and her slippers drop, left then right.

It's all right now to free her,
now as she lies on the bed
and stares at the ceiling.
Does she wonder, I wonder,
what that steady knocking is?
If I could, I'd tell her it's me
sounding the walls of her body

in search of a way back in.

*

Aloha, 'Āina

i

My father knocked
my mother up early
in March, maybe

it was late
February. Had it been
a leap year

my conception might have been
miraculous. But no,
it was the year

of the Ram.
Kierkegaard and Nietzsche
had long since died

and my home, one of eight
islands, was still
a territory, not a state.

In '59 statehood took the "i"
from reality leaving us
only real estate.

I left in '74.

ii

One by one the trees fall—
sandalwood, *kiawe* and now
the *'ōhi'a*, whose blossoms

I dared not pluck as a child
lest rain, more rain, fall
by my own hand.

Not even the palm,
shading its fruits' dark husk and
milk-white core, is safe.

I don't need to hear the tree fall
to feel it. I know nature
abhors a vacuum.

With each felled tree,
new displacements: tonight
the wake of its wind

driven across the Pacific
and falling, cold and black as rain,
even here, far away as I live.

*

The Hollow

. . . *an eaten live thing.*
—Marilyn Nelson

When its heart breaks
through the slats
of its rib cage

how can it cry out?

Without a heart, a hurt
thing's tongue and lips
lose their feel for plosives,

fricatives, glottal stops.

Its breath.
The hollow that wells
in its heart's stead

is a brooding silence

hurt things know.
Silence is its own space.
My grandma's word

for space is *ma*.

Know *ma*, she says.
It teaches that
nothing comforts.

*

Proteus

Licked by the tongues of sleep
we dream of birth, of water
seeking the lowest way. No matter
we cease to feel the staunch heart
beating. Out of darkness the spirit
is thrust and made to breathe deep,

and as it breathes in the deep
expanses of space, it ceases to sleep.
As if sure of other spirits
it swims or treads water
in an ocean where the heart
is an island where everything matters.

The thought that everything is matter
is a thought so darkly deep
it tangles the veins and arteries of the heart
into knots, undone only by sleep.
Dreams of clear blue salty water
and ancient fish hint of spirit,

but the idea that everything is spirit
also harrows dreams: it matters
that the parched body cries out, "Water!"
Awake, unable to drink deep
enough at the wellspring of sleep,
it fears the throb of its thirsting heart.

Some dark secret bars the heart
against the small fist of spirit
banging on the doors of sleep.
There is no grasping the matter.
Whatever it is lies deep,
seethes pure and clear as water;

under the skin there is only water,
surging and piercing the heart
like a blade driven hard and deep
through whatever thick caul the spirit
wears. Do these brief lives matter?
Is there more to death than sleep?

Blood, blood, water of spirit,
this is the heart of the matter:
cell deep, we cannot deny sleep.

*

Heal-All: In Memory of Kana Nakama

Just carry on an ordinary task without attachments.
—Rinzai

Because the sky is a cipher
above the acre my new house stands on,

walking among nameless objects,
I test the few names I've learned:

loblolly, quince, heal-all,
names on my lips

still more real
than the greenness in my hand.

I clip dead wood from a rosebush,
prune new growth from the gangly hedge.

Tonight, I know, I'll open my books once more,
for someone has already named the flora,

and because with words and photographs
my mother will want to know

what grows here. But now it's time
to face what's absent, and give ground

to what's near at hand. Here
the memory of how to move past grief

in the pungent remains
of last year's leaves,

clearer than any words or photographs:
you, Grandmother, raking wet leaves

in your yard, the rhythm of work
your measure of silence,

and later, your voice,
trailing your sure steps toward the kitchen,

saying, "Eat. And get some sun,"
by which you mean to tell me

I've grown too pale and thin.

*

Immigrants

To be always carrying
this stone whose own inertia
keeps doubling its weight even

as I hold it in my hand—
in truth I would cast it off
if I could
          though it cool the
sweat of my palm, suffer it-
self to be touched. Know I would

heft it at water or glass
simply to hear one thing
deafen another awake

to hear fragments falling like
stars to wound or baptize
everything
          compassed inside
the arc of its wake—but for
one thing: my grandmother gave

this stone to my mother, and
she to me, saying each hand
need have something hard to fill

its grasping, something only
time and touch can transmute in-
to an object,
          beautiful,
this stone from Okinawa
where the grains of sand are stars.

*

PART TWO: The Corsage

Obake

Once late at night I saw *Obāsan*
come out of her room.
She thumped her cane softly
down the moon-dim hall.
Her bedpan scraped against the hardwood floor
as she slid it with her tabi-covered foot
toward the bathroom door.

She turned slowly to face me.
Her wrinkly lips whispered something
I did not understand.
Her electric hair glowed white.

But then she was rising and swelling all around me,
drowning out the light.
And no one knew she had swallowed me up
in the mazy print of her black-and-white kimono.

So now when we hear the sirens at school
and push our desks against the windows,
it's her scrape-and-thump I hear.
As I kneel, then bow,
then hold my head down with my hands,
it's her I'm hiding from.

*

Marginalia: Honolulu, 1970

The teacher kept saying, "Pay
attention," and I had been, only
elsewhere, my thoughts like trapped birds
in search of an open window.

Her voice—how can I say this
kindly?—was like the hum
of an overworked refrigerator,
constant and keeping things cold.

The girl next to me kept up
a furious scribble, occasionally
looking up, "paying attention"
while under her right hand a line

of flowers softened the left margin
of her college-ruled paper.
The teacher turned her back to us;
I reached over and penciled

a neat *aloha* in a four-petaled flower,
the one "a" doing double duty,
become alpha and omega,
the word an immortal snake.

In the margin, the girl sketched
the teacher's face and under it wrote
Mongoose. Outside the window,
thick clouds were gathering over Punchbowl.

for Annette Keli'ikoa

*

Spheres of Influence

Under a full moon, Mother,
you and your old friend chant
the names of the moon's other phases—
gibbous, quarter, crescent, new.
Your bodies tremble with laughter,
touch at the broad points of shoulder
and hip. You guess how many puppies
there will be. A slight breeze rattles
the brittle leaves, hangs the odor
of ripening mango and lychee
heavily on the humid air.
A mango thumps beside the dogs.
Do the bitch's haunches hurt
in the vice grip of those awkward paws?
Your friend wraps an arm around you,
lifts the other to name and show you
a star: Aldebaran, the Bull's eye.
His lips round, seal, and part
in talk of supernovas and white
dwarfs—words impenetrable
as that mass of clouds racing
past the moon. The bitch's eyes
glare a terrifying green.
Remember how Kuro steadied
a lychee between his paws
this afternoon, severed
the prickly shell with his teeth,
mouthed the fleshy white pulp
and dropped the pit? How
last month, you drew small circles
on the kitchen calendar to explain
my body's impulse toward ripeness:
crescent, quarter, gibbous, full.

*

With My Mother and Aunts in the Kitchen

While the rest of us watch a football game,
they talk story over butterrolls, palm leaves, and coffee.
My father and uncles sip beer.
In low voices my mother and aunts talk.

All four of them laugh; their laughter,
like the sound of the cheering crowd,
washes over the drone of the sportscaster.
I want to join them in the kitchen.

They end their talk about so-and-so;
the youngest summing it up is all I hear:
"One married woman out li' dat till t'ree?"

My aunt who calls my mother Ann,
not Nan or Nancy, calls me

niele, Miss Nosy, Miss Big Ears
and nods a smile in my direction.
The others (even my mother) laugh.
My aunt hands me her empty cup.
I fill it.

No one tells me to go,
so I sit in the empty chair and listen.

in memory of Alice Sagawinit

*

Calling from the Gate

Mother stops scouring the rice pot
and wipes red hands on the hem
of her shirt. She picks up the salt-
shaker, to take to Grandmother,
who stands calling from the gate:
"Tsuneko! Tsuneko!"

                         Mother clicks
on the porch light and steps out
beyond its reach. She sprinkles
salt into Grandmother's cupped hand.
Grandmother takes the salt up by pinchfuls
and casts it back, over her shoulders.
Having just come from a funeral,
she will not let unfamiliar spirits
enter the home of her kin.

                         *

New Year's Eve

The night our mothers
turned us loose with Zippo lighters
and a string of firecrackers,
we raced to the back stairs.
We dared each other
to hold those red devils
till the count of five,
like heroes with grenades
in old war movies—
certain no fuse
would last past three.

My tag-along sister
and her friend traced
their names with sparklers
out in front. Stuck in cold water,
the spent rods hissed.
A hot hand of *hana*
flared in the kitchen,
hoots and groans burst out
as players slapped cards down.
Long into the night
they chunked ice cubes
into glasses, filled
empty beer cases
with bottles sweating still.

In the glow of yellow light
I plucked at my string
and secretly counted—
he loves me, he loves me not—
as we tossed fireworks
whose shattered shells

would blanket the lawn
like a thousand hibiscus petals,
before the new year dawned.

*

Back to Back

At sixteen my mother had been a swimmer.
I have seen a picture of her

poised at the edge of the pool, knees bent,
hands on knees, and smiling with her teammates.

My aunt once said back then she swam
as gracefully as Esther Williams.

But that is not how I remember her.
It is when I am sixteen and a runner

and am forever wanting to stand against her,
back to back, to see who's taller;

however much I stretch I still come up
an inch short. I've called her up

to have her drive me home from practice.
We ride home in utter silence

after my curt "thanks" and her nod,
not for lack of feeling, but for want of words.

Following her in, cleats slung over my shoulder,
I tell her to wait, I'll help her.

Already she's at the sink, peeling potatoes
and humming, one foot lifted like a flamingo.

*

The Corsage

I stood in front of the fridge,
door ajar, unable to decide whether
to leave my first corsage

where it lay or take it out,
but then I realized the answer
to my dilemma required no thought:

all I had to do was stand there
to save and hold it, too. I held
the corsage all of five minutes before

your grandmother got impatient,
said, "You're letting all the cold
air out. Will you get what you want?!"

So I decided. In my room
I gently touched the flower's
face, daydreamed about him.

Remembering the evening, the dance,
I studied the orchid's features,
discovered...odd resemblances.

On my neck I could feel his breath
as he was pinning the corsage carefully
so as not to touch my breast.

Out along the walk a bee
lost itself in the orchid briefly
then started chasing me toward his Chevy.

Leaving home then, what did I know? I've read
that ancient Greeks named the flower orchid
because its roots look like testicles, orchis.

Fifteen years ago I forgave him
for enlisting in the Army as soon
as school let out that June.

The corsage, what of it remains,
is here. The orchid withered, fern
and spray of baby's breath turned

brown and brittle. What do I care?
This satin ribbon with its fine edging
is still as elegant as the costly underwear

I had bought just for that evening
and had lost somewhere between leaving
and returning to the house my parents lived in.

*

Courage, Temperance, and Wisdom

Lord, when shall we be done changing?
—Melville

Dear Annette: Sixteen years ago our mothers
were not much older than we are now.
God, how we hated their stupidity
and submissiveness and swore we'd not repeat
the pattern of their lives. We'd be ourselves.
So, of course, we had to join the Air Force.
(I still owe you one for that.) I think
my folks have finally forgiven me
for ruining the family reputation.
Two weeks after my eighteenth birthday
I signed my own enlistment papers,
saw you off at the airport, then waited
one very long month for my time to come.
Back then I thought I was leaving home
for good. On the one-stop flight from Hawai'i
to Texas and Basic Training, ocean
yielded to land, and the islands I saw
were lakes. I've never gotten over it.
At Lackland I learned a new way to fold
my underwear. I wrote letters to Brad
under the covers by flashlight. Don't say,
"How romantic." You know, I wrote a couple
that way to my mother, too. It may be
that distance is all. And I have walked
a long time in my mother's zoris, spanked, scowled
and scolded my own child into submission
almost against my will—"for his own good."
Is all this old news? My eyes hurt. Sometimes
I think this pursuit of philosophy
is likely to give me only words for things
my mother had already taught me.
For us, dinner was always a lesson

in courage, temperance, and wisdom: she'd heap
eggplant, spinach, broccoli, or some green thing
on my plate and say, "Eat," and after,
a stingy scoop of ice cream—always serving
her husband with her children. For Brad and me
it's the standard joke: "Your arm broke or what?"
It doesn't always work. I guess you know
what that's about. Lately I've begun
to wonder which way is better: to serve
or not to serve. Well, there's the rub. Perhaps
it's because I have no daughters to raise.
Even now I sometimes half expect you
and your girls, pillows and blankets in hand,
to turn up unexpectedly at some
ungodly hour, and you asking me,
"You got something to eat?" as you did
last year during your break from school;
while Brad and the kids slept, we chewed
the fat. Al too, you quipped, had gone remote.
But Missoula is just a bit farther
from Buffalo than Storrs is, and phone calls
and letters are sorry substitutes.
Is it really over between you, then?
Me ke aloha pumehana, Kang.

*

Island Fever

Here where it is always summer
breath is almost never visible.
Rain falls even in summer.
Sidewalks hiss.

Seen from a fifth-floor window
of the Amfac building,
the harbor is pretty.

Five o'clock. *Time's up*,
says the clock.
Elevators rise
then fall with the weight of bodies.
Outside glass doors
it's hot, the light hurts.

Seen from rolled-down windows
of cars weaving
the narrow descent
into valleys,
the sun suggests
its diurnal rounds,
an eye,
closing, opening.

From the doorway
a stretched shadow touches the leg
of a table. It bends
to take off its shoes.
The floor creaks.
On the table, two stones—
one gray, one black—
click against each other.
A chair's legs creak.

Someone sits at the table
pressing the tips of thumbs and fingers
of opposite hands together.
It could be prayer.
She stares at the stones.

She touches them.
She likes the feel of them.

She picks up
the black one,
the one worn smooth by water.

I hold it against my forehead.

*

In the Way Back

One must go around for news of home.
—Japanese proverb

The Friday before Labor Day
after a day's hard work
my father'd come home, read the paper
then tell my mother:
"Mo' bettah take da kids around da island."

Next morning, up early, mother'd be
telling us to turn off the TV
and packing a picnic lunch:
musubi, scrambled eggs, Spam,
a thermos of watered-down Exchange.

Stuck in the way back of the Valiant
I faced the closed rear window
already hot, thinking how much
I hated this.
At my back my grandma sat,
next to her my brother and sisters dozed.
In front of them my parents sat,
in front of them the long way back.
My mother drove.
Beside her on the seat,
the lunch she'd packed.
My father hung an elbow out the window.

Out of the city and into "scenery"
that blurred ocean, sand and trees,
I pulled out my pack of cards
and played solitaire. My shuffling woke
my sister. She reached past
the back of the front seat
to turn on the radio.

Back in her seat she reached behind
and tapped me on the shoulder.
She leaned and whispered,
"Having one good time already?"
She laughed and climbed
into the way back.

                    And then
we were four kids laughing
and singing in the way back
with the Rascals, "How Can I Be Sure?"
and Bill Withers, "Lean on Me"
while in between
my grandma sang the chorus:
"*Matte, matte* you, damn kids,
look the view!"
which sounded to us kids like
"Rook the few."

And in between the singing and the laughing
one of us kept asking,
"We stay dere or what?"
all the way to Hau-ʻula Beach
where Grandma smoked a cigarette
and gathered stones along the shore.

The rest of us ate silently.
And silently when we were done
we piled into the car. My father drove,
slowing or stopping now and again to show us
the Crouching Lion,
Chinaman's Hat,
the Blow Hole,
Koko Head, Diamond Head
then Honolulu after dark.
As if he meant to tell us:
When you let the island in you
the road both does and doesn't lead you back.

Four kids in the way back of the Valiant
leaning one upon the other,
we didn't have to watch the road.
Our parents left us free to look in both directions,
behind us and ahead.

for my father

*

PART THREE: Homing Pidgin

Bruises

My father's life is the sound of one hand
clapping. Against his body a stepfather
lifted an open hand or fist. His mother
drank hard liquor and smoked unfiltered Camels.
He sealed himself shut like a safe. And I, the son
who steadied the boot as he fixed its heel, or
handed tools to a hand reaching from under
the Ford—what's the use? How can I imagine

a life where history doesn't repeat itself?
A daughter grown tired of using my head
to make the sound of two hands clapping, myself
bruising the air with words that strike at nothing, dead
to what it was nourished by—no. I must try. This left
hand, held out, makes the sound of one hand clapping. Listen.

*

Smoke

Her hands are pasty and liver-spotted,
one nesting in her denim apron,
thumb and index finger of the other

pinching the end of a cigarette
and touching her lips. She takes a long drag
through the butcher-paper filter

she's fashioned herself. All of her
up from the backs of her knees,
thighs, buttocks, even the small of her back

touches the straight-backed chair in the dim room,
smoke from the cigarette she's just killed
hazing the air like an old pool hall's.

For a moment, Korea rises from the ashes.
I can see it in the way her body reposes
against the chair's hardness. "Tell me,

Grandma, did you take up those cigarettes
because you could not send back home in letters
the words you spoke?"

Eyes clouded by cataracts, she leans
toward my voice. The only word I make out
among the guttural mumbling that is

her native tongue: "Camels."

*

In My Father's House

In my father's house, for as long as I remember, beer
Has always been a man's drink. One New Year's Eve, my mother
And her sisters gathered in the kitchen, drinking highballs
Instead of coffee. They'd closed the door, a momentary wall
Between themselves and their men and children. It was after dinner.

And once my uncle came careening through the front door
Then passed out. I hid behind the sofa till my mother
Got him to his feet. He said, "I'm drunk as a monkey's uncle,"
In my father's house.

In my father's yard there's a lychee tree. For many years
Insects laid dark clusters of eggs on its leaves. Last year my father
Cut its branches off, then tarred the stumps. Tonight no rattle
Of leaves, no sweet fruit. I sit in his yard nursing a bottle.
It's hot. I helped myself to what I knew would not be offered,
In my father's house.

*

Pineapples

Back where I come from
they call my father's people Yobo, kimchee,
the Irish of the East. I have heard
my father fuming under his breath,
and caught my own self
frothing, and might confirm it.

Though I've never been called by those names,
I have been called Nit, which
on a good day, I might identify as a sort of changeling
from rice to lice to Nit
rather than Nippon to Nip to Nit.

My Grandma Lee, a picture bride at sixteen,
was a hard woman from Seoul
who birthed her first six children
on a sugar plantation in Kō-loa.
I trace her presence in the Aloha State
back to King Ka-lā-kaua's invitation.

You could not tell from the fact of her thirteen children
that her life was a series of refusals.
For five years she shared a bedroom
with my sister and me, refusing
our pidgin English, telling my father
Japanese girls are no good.
Then she went to live with her daughter.
What else could she do?
Besides, my mother's true tribe is the hairy Okinawan.

Once, in a rage, my mother's father
dragged two of his daughters back to their rooms
for dating *haoles*. My mother remembers waking

to their screams. They both married locals.
But I, I married a *haole*,
and my father all but disowned me.

And now, what do I think I am?
Call me Yobo, call me Nit,
call me a hairy Okinawan
and I do not flinch.
What should I do—hate myself?

Out of the common soil that claimed
my grandparents' bones, I have risen,
sweet island home, surrounded by ocean,
place of my origins. My given name
is Pineapple—a native,
trueborn, if not indigenous—
a truth, a home
some would deny me.

Tell me Hawai'i is not my home
and watch me explode.

for Garrett Hongo

*

Wild Horse Island

My father stabled wild horses
in his heart. At least that's
what he told me. In my mind
hey and *hay* became synonymous.

So when he opened the first
of a six-pack he had me
bring him after supper,
I always believed

I was feeding his horses.
On my tenth birthday,
midway through his fifth,
he pulled me up on his lap

in the living room.
We watched TV.
Soon I felt the dead weight
of his big arm begin

to squeeze my shoulders together.
Though wired on sugar from soft
drinks and Hostess cupcakes,
I stared at the TV, fretting

about my nonexistent breasts.
Like my twelve-year molars,
I thought, and wisdom teeth,
they were fully formed

but hidden. What,
I wondered, what if
they got impacted, or worse,
turned inside out and pushed out

on my back? Afraid to wake him,
I stiffened my elbows, hollowed my chest
against the pressure till, exhausted,
all I could do was give in

and drowse between the flares
and explosions from the screen.
My father's flinches were horses' hooves,
his erratic breathing horses snorting

or peeing. My father woke
when they played the National Anthem.
He turned off the TV.
"Five dead soldiers," he said to the fridge,

"and one still cold."

for Lee Evans

*

Homing Pidgin

i

Smoked-glass highrises
paling the business district
spare me the sight of
the sunset, another coin
pocketed in paradise.

ii

"Take pictures," you said.
But how could I take pictures
and fish, too? I fished
until I couldn't fish. Here.
Pictures of the waves and cliffs.

iii

Palani Vaughn sang
as his daughter danced hula
under the Dog Star.
When he stopped—words echoing
the ocean's redundance still yet.

iv

Kālua puʻa,
haupia, Primo and *poi*.
Laulau, *lūʻau* leaves,
lomilomi salmon. O,
I t'ink dees mus' be heaven.

*

No *Pilikia*; or, Piece of Cake

Hele mai, have one beer,
Da bossman he wen' go take one break.
Eh, brah, no *pilikia*.

I been married for seventeen years.
I met my old lady Ala Moana Beach Park.
I wen' said, Us go have one beer.

T'ree months later she almost bite off my ear.
See da scar? She *huhū* 'cuz I wen' take
Another *wahine* out. But no *pilikia*.

She told me she wen' soak her pillow with tears
Till I wen' send her flowers and make
one note li' dees: Can we have a beer?

See, I wen' go look in the mirror.
You not getting no younger, I wen' t'ink.
Two week later I wen' marry her. No *pilikia*.

So no *pilikia* about one little fight, brah.
Just go King's Bakery, take her one cake.
Eh, finish your beer,
 I no like no *pilikia*.

for Uncle Jimmy

*

Hawaiian Time

What time stay?

According to my skin getting darker—

Eh, I pack
pine so can go
holoholo, buy
pakalolo, watch
TV. No waste
time make joke,
old man. What
time stay?

Waste time, you.
Before time
stay home talk story,
chug-a-lug
'ōkolehao, eat *pupus*,
play
slack key kine cha-lang-a-lang.
Only good fun.

Old fut, what
time stay?

According to my skin,
getting darker.

Eh, old man,
whatever. *Make*, die
dead. Same smell.
What time stay?

Pau hana time.

Come again?

Five o'clock.

Thanks, eh?

No make mention.

*

Taproot

Stooping to pull up a weed,
I think of my father
who made of weeding an art.

After work, he'd take a bucket
and his weeder from the toolshed
and clear an area of a yard he knew

would never look manicured,
whose quality would, at best,
be like something homemade.

He'd set the bucket upside down
and sit on it. Plotting a route
he'd shift the bucket, a move

so deft you might think he was just
leaning out to extend his reach.
He knew exactly where and what angle

to drive the weeder down,
north and south of the weed,
without severing its taproot.

When my father worked like this,
making small mounds he'd later
gather up in his bucket,

the dog would sniff at his bare feet
then lie down in the shade his body made.
Grounded there, he was most himself,

his hunger for perfection and control
giving way, finally, to the work itself.
It was easy to love him then.

*

Syllabus

Steering between
Scylla and Charybdis
—it's all a dream

at the top of the spine,
that reptilian brain

(ontogeny
still recapitulates
phylogeny)—

o, soup to nuts! the same
chaos, chaos rattling bones

in the attic
as some old house settles.
I don't panic.

Ancients steering by star
charts, wave patterns went far

though once I roamed
among ruins and found
nobody home.

Death, breath; death, breath my foot-
fall echoed down the street.

Remembering
the mariner, bone ragged,
dead drunk, swearing

by God, "From womb to tomb
we're fucked and far from home,"

I pray for grace
and forgetfulness, this
rockandhard place

so be it: the lame tongue
curling itself on *love*,

dull metronome
marking time till it turn:
Iamb. Iamb. I am.

for Patricia Goedicke

*

PART FOUR: Catch and Release

Fishing the Sky

Through the lens of time-
lapse photography,
I picture the moon

blinking off sleep. All month
I've been waiting.

When the sun hesitates

on a mountain peak,
I stand on my porch

to watch it draw
the night behind it

like a shade. The lights

from the town below me
come on, a false dawn.

*

Last month I imagined
one of my neighbor's cows
kicking mulish heels

as the full moon rose.
I imagined myself
trailing my fingers

through light solid
as water, casting lines
falling in graceful arcs—

at home in the bowl
of the Dipper, the lap
of the Great Bear.

*

Tonight the sky is
overcast. I can't

see my own hand.
Darkness is tangible

as the porch rail
under my hand. I
can almost believe

if I stood on the rail

and leaned my full weight
into the night, like the wind
at Pali Lookout,

darkness would hold me.

*

Without the Bear
I can't measure my way

to the North Star.
For all I know I could

be on a ship's deck
at sea. From where I stand

the stars I cannot see
glow cold, indifferent

and white. Satellite dishes
pan the sky like beacons.

If I cup my ears
with my hands, I can almost
hear their motors hum.

*

Becoming One of the Guys

Holloman AFB, New Mexico

When he said my thigh was nothing like his girlfriend's,
There was a world of innocence in it.
I'd been sitting on the workbench, self-absorbed,
Bumping the heels of my combat boots

Against the cabinets when he tumbled in,
Half drunk, and struggled to close the latch.
Next thing I knew he'd taken my hand,
Lain his head on my lap and stretched

Out beside me. That was when he said it.
It startled the rest of the guys on shift,
Who till then imagined me a sort of holy virgin
Beyond touch. His one act made me human

And later, before we left Holloman,
Those Texans risked sneaking me into their hut
To celebrate our return to Bergstrom
With beers, chips, and several hands of hearts.

But that night, where else had he to go? Alcohol
Could not relieve his sense of separateness
Nor make the ghost he was then less real.
And there on deployment, we all felt homeless,

At night in some desert in New Mexico.
Though he seemed out of place in his civvies—
Jeans, plaid shirt, and cowboy boots—how
Could we tell him he shouldn't be with us?

We sat and waited, my arm rising and falling
With his steady breathing, so like the waters I turned
Away from, two years before, in leaving the islands.
Until Rick stood, shook him and whispered,

"Dave, wake up, you best head on back to the hut."

*

Distance

I've begun to acquire a taste
for country and western, driving
the forty-mile stretch between here
and the Garden City. The whine of my engine
winding the long hills up and down through
the Bitterroot Valley and that slight trembling
my car does when I get it up past
fifty-five are intoxicating.
Who needs beer? Emmylou Harris comes on
and I'm humming and next thing I know
I'm crying—though whether for what I've left
behind or where I'm going or both
I can't be certain. Sometimes I feel
I should just keep going. I adjust
my rearview mirror. In it I watch my life
or work, depending on which way I'm headed,
swim out of sight. In that blur
the yellow line on the pavement reminds me
of monofilament, and I'm thinking fish
or cut bait. But I still can't figure out
which end of the line I'm holding. Some days
this love of words seems little more than self-
love or unfaithfulness to what in this world
I love. Is there no reconciling them?
Six months ago I thought I put those doubts to rout.
My heart festers, a sore that will not bear
touch. And so to stave off self-pity
I hammer out poems that partake
of the hard and icy perfection of diamonds.
I'm still struggling to gain
some useful perspective. You know
last month my eye doctor told me to keep
the page at arm's length when I read and take
some time to focus on things at a distance.
He said my eye muscles, the ones that tense

and make me increasingly myopic, need time
to relax. I've been taking some time
to look out through all of my windows.
Last week five does, their steps uncertain and jerky,
crossed my neighbor's pasture not fifty yards
from my kitchen window. From that same window
two weeks ago I'd seen, for the first time,
two calves, despite their awkward bulk, frisking
like kittens. No kidding. Given all
that space and shrunken by distance, I guess,
to me their stiffness assumed a kind of grace.
And that same week, driving back from the city
I chased a black bear, come down to the lower end
of Smith Creek Lane for windfall apples,
up a ponderosa pine. Our first week here,
back in September, we'd seen sign of him
heaped in our apple orchard—and now
there he was, taking a second to stand upright
and squint through my headlights before
lowering himself on all fours and turning to the tree.
Already it's November. Today I faced
a blank page at arm's length, taking some time
to stare out at the autumn sky. I am
a hunter watching the cold, gray sky
from behind a duck blind, waiting
for black marks to push through the blankness
of sky. This is a metaphor you gave me,
one that I dwell on and now give back.

to Greg Pape

*

Catch and Release

I should have remembered
what the Japanese know:
there are moments

the whole body is one
sense, when even the lightest
touch is dangerous.

I should have but didn't
remember when, instead of my usual
nod of acknowledgment,

I took the hand he offered.
We could have been lovers holding hands,
he, a stout, balding man,

and I, still looking pubescent.
My age surprised him, to hear him tell it,
and as he spoke of the trout he caught

and released, gesturing how with both hands
he held it to fill its gills with water,
knowing the shock of both acts

had probably injured it,
I should have remembered.
It was alcohol brought him perilously close

to crying for the fish, and the drink
he lifted to his lips that kept him from it.
If, as Plato tells us, all love begins

with physical attraction, what am I
to make of that moment between us,
the handshake we parted with

now numbered among my losses.

*

World Enough

Because there is time,
I shall pull my student desk outside, in sunlight,
and though new to these parts, instinctively recognize
the call of a catbird. But first
I'll lean into the face of Bashō, my cat, for luck;
while on my hands and knees on the kitchen floor
I shall praise him because he never licks my face
and promise to turn my cheek the next time
he runs the length of his body against my forehead and stops
with his uplifted stub of a tail in my face.
I shall listen to trapped insects buzz and plink
against the screen on my screened-in porch.
I shall let the phone ring.
I shall take time to remember that just last week
the oak tree sprouted feathers,
and notice the tent caterpillar blown by on a silver thread,
the oak's shadow already a snowflake.
I shall watch the wind rock the pear tree's celery stalk of a trunk
and wish I'd gone outside when the tree snowed petals last week.
I shall take a catnap.
Surprised by the effort it makes to cough down its one note,
I shall study the crow perched on the pole supporting the mercury-vapor light.
I shall remember, watching it,
the long month as, frantic to finish my thesis on Hawthorne,
I walked to my office after supper to try to write—
always at dusk a great-horned owl atop a ponderosa pine
not twenty yards from my window, the ceremonial bowing,
its body growing invisible as the night echoed with its one clear note.
I shall ask myself what studying Hawthorne has given me.
After staring a long time
past the greening hydrangea I thought was dead,
my answer shall be, "A lot."
I shall see steam lift off my shadow's head because my hair is—
Stop. You've letters to write and a house that begs cleaning—
still I *can* clear a space

the way each spring others work ground for a flower garden
and remind myself in the face of the daily business of living,
there is always a habitable place,
the farthest outpost of solitude nothing can touch,
where there is time, there is always time.

*

On the Eve of My Thirty-fifth Birthday

Surely joy is the condition of life.
—Thoreau

I do not think I'll dye
these few gray hairs on my head
black to hide my decay;
instead, I'll let them go

white to bare my nakedness. Adam
and Eve tried to hide it
and look what God did.
Before I knew man-

kind and *No* was the word
I bit my tongue on, I too
was innocent. No,
I will go

as I am. I see the prick
and pain of it,
the sharp sting, for what
it is. How else

could I have come
to know where death resides,
how know the tongue that speaks?
Then, of course, I did not

know the word was also *know*.
But now, yes, I will say
it was good. Here,
nearing the end

of a century,
where nothing seems to last,
all I want
is to know the Architect

of erections that will last.

*

Prothalamion:
Of My Brother in Los Angeles

For the Romans, one test of a man's faith
was stretching his neck for the barber.
And there he was, on the verge of falling

into the chair a second time. On the eve
of the wedding, he was saying, "I can't
get real excited about this." Maybe

it was easier the first time, for a boy
still in his twenties. Finding him
after ten years wandering, I found myself

amazed as, again and again, his words rang
like an oracle's; he talked of Miles Davis
and Shirley Horn, of our generation's music

and the Spin Doctors, of loving
best musicians who take as their task
finding their own way

to build on the classics. Knowing him then,
woman to man, could I love men
who make no room in their lives for music?

But I admit when we were teens
sometimes through walls and ceilings
the upper registers of his scales

and improvisations sounded to me
like squeaky doors and car horns.
Night and day. And then one day

he'd be riding a clear note,
a pearl diver going deep and deeper,
turned back only by the need to breathe;

and yet, he'd fall into the tune, this time
his play unmuddied by the need to backtrack.
I asked him, "Are you happy?" He just smiled

and started singing, *Don't you know
when your lovin' anybody, baby,
you're taking a gamble on a little sorrow,*

and damned if I'm not singing,
Honey, get it while you can.

*

Fidelity

Maybe it was the temperature
        rising from twenty-five to fifty in a few hours,
        or the snowplows traded in for mowers and mulchers.
Maybe it was the college kids in jams and T-shirts
        sunning themselves or playing with Frisbees,
        or the furrows bicycle tires made in the oozy mud.
Maybe it was this made me think us back to high school
        and remember something Vosberg said. Remember Vosberg?
        Goatee, bald head, polka-dotted bow ties?
Maybe he was right. Maybe he knew
        what he was talking about after all
        when out of the blue, one day, he told our class:
"Maybe *fuck* comes from the German *pflug*,
        which means 'plow,' and not *ficken*,
        which means 'to strike,' as is commonly held."
Maybe this was how I came to think of
        knocked up, banged up, screwed, fucked.
        What had they to do with love?
Maybe this was how I came to think of
        making love, making babies, sleeping together,
        and how each, in its own way, entails a little death.
Maybe it was this made me come to recognize
        that though we have no mind to make more babies,
        part of our love making is simply sleeping / together.
Maybe it was this made me want to write to tell you:
        Tonight I'll hold this emptiness inside me,
        counting the ways I've slept with you, like sheep.

*

Blue Apartments

In the dry season he will come down from the mountain
Bear will come down with the deer
who come down to graze above Green Hill
at the base of the mountain

It will be dark

He will come down from the mountain
his cream-colored face
like the full moon coming down from the hill
to the swings where I wait
with a glass of ice water
while he lifts one short leg over the rubber
the curved seat gloving his hind end like a loincloth
as he settles in
sideways
one chain aligning itself down the length of his spine

then he will prop his right foot high on the other
bend and unbend his left knee
as he studies the parked cars
the lot's wavering lights
the blue apartments'
muted voices

After a while I will offer him
the glass of water
hear his right foot pad softly in the dirt
his claws clink against the glass
as he struggles to fish an ice cube from it
feel the dry air moisten
as he leans forward tilting the small mouth of the glass
toward me

I will dip the whole of my hand in it
then hold an ice cube out to him
Using his claws like chopsticks
he will lift the melting ice cube from my palm

And after a while I will tell him
how I spent a whole day
at the Honolulu Zoo
how after the talking-bird show
after coaxing a peacock to display
after the lion declared its presence with one loud roar
and the tired monkeys
hung their chins on the grid of their cages
it was the grizzly I turned to
resting my forearms
on the top bar of the chainlink fence
gradually leaning beyond it
the whole afternoon
the bear in his doorway
like Diogenes
absorbing the warmth and light

I will tell him how that bear
sitting on the concrete slab of his doorway
also propped his right foot up
and for a moment with our eyes closed
the world was beautifully red

I will tell him that was twenty years ago
and though embarrassed I will tell him
where I live
He will lift me from the swing
and ascend the stairs to my apartment

I will ask him to stay
the night

*

Because I Could Not Go Home for My Aunt's Funeral

because my mother's parents were immigrants
and she was one of eight children, an elder girl child,
because she fell into mothering while herself still a child,
because in two years' time she's lost her mother and two
of three baby sisters, because she'll be sixty-four and is learning
time is no longer on her side, but mostly because it is
one of the few things she cannot teach herself, I teach my mother
to ride a bicycle. We get the old bicycle out of the shed
and dust off the orange frame, banana seat, and stingray
handlebars. The weather is fine, a typical day with a little
liquid sunshine, as we are used-to to saying,
and we're in front of the house on Prospect Street.
I check the brakes, remembering how at ten
I couldn't quite bring myself to jam the pedals backward at first,
and so the first few times I stopped myself by steering
straight into the hibiscus hedge. I pull a few wheelies, pull up
to my mother; she's saying, *Lunch* and *Laundry*. Holding
a handlebar and the back of the seat, I say, *Get on.*
We move slowly at first, she wagging the handlebars
and dropping and lifting a foot to some crazy beat
that jars out my pleas: *Don't / worry—I'll / hold the / bicycle / up*
—though we both know I will strain against her full weight.
We must look like close cousins to clowns with an oversized tricycle.
But it doesn't take long. She loosens her grip on the bars
and her whole body relaxes, and I am jogging alongside,
my hand lightly resting behind her on the seat, and saying, *Brake,*
practice using the brake. I sit on the U-shaped cement block
cupping the fire hydrant near her parked car as she makes passes
back and forth in front of me. Once she puts her feet up
on the well of the handlebars, once she lets them go, and twice
she puts her feet up and lets the handlebars go.
Without warning she speeds past me saying, *Watch,*
then glances back as if it were something she'd always
wanted to do but needs to ask, *Okay?* I'm up on my feet
waving her forward and running toward San Antonio Avenue.

From the corner I watch her. Feet perfectly stanced
on the pedals, hands on the bars to steady the front wheel,
she coasts down the hill, poised, a surfer riding the big wave.

*

The Weep Line

Under the trees we paced
and drove Jobe's spikes
along the weep line.
Working clear of roots,
I held the spikes
while you hammered.
I kept looking up at
the trees because,
until rain falls
heavy and steady,
we must imagine it.
Later, when it appears,
an imperfect circle
under the pin oak,
I think of you, still
a child among grade-school
children holding hands,
forming a circle. Caught

*

outdoors in a downpour
you step inside the weep line.
Leaves on the tree's upper
branches sluice rain down.
Under the tree you can hear
rain drop, leaf by leaf, down to
the weep line. Beyond it
everything's hazy. I know
you think life's like that.
There, under the tallest tree,
here, where often lightning
strikes close by, you know
by now life's currency, and—
if you're the man

I think you are—
you'll also imagine
the spikes, now unseen,
feeding the tree.

for my son David on his 18th birthday

*

Notes

p. 20   The phrase *aloha ʻāina*, which means "love of the land," was popularized in the mid-1970s by the Project Kahoʻolawe ʻOhana movement. The *ʻōhiʻa* blossoms are called *lehua*; in island folklore it is believed that picking the blossoms would bring rain—a belief that may be rooted in a Hawaiian myth. In a fit of jealousy, Pele, goddess of volcanoes, destroyed her favorite younger sister Hiʻi-aka's *lehua* and *hala* groves and inflicted terrible suffering on Hōpoe, Hiʻi-aka's beloved mortal companion.

p. 31   In Japanese folklore, *obake* are female spirits who haunt crossroads. In Hawaiʻi, Japanese mothers used the word the way their mainland counterparts used the word *bogeyman*. *Obasan* is an honorific term for an elder female; here it refers to my great-grandmother.

p. 35   Tsuneko is my mother's Japanese name. It means "common child."

p. 42   *Me ke aloha pumehana* means "with warm aloha."

p. 45   Another name for *musubi* is *onigiri*. It is rice pressed into a triangular shape and wrapped with dried seaweed.

p. 46   *Matte* is the imperative form of the Japanese verb meaning "to wait."

p. 54   Yobo, a racial epithet depending on who's saying it, comes from Yoboseo, which is what Koreans call themselves.

p. 58   The fourth section is comprised of a list of foods, the names of which are intended to stand in for the pleasure of the foods themselves. *Puʻa* is the contracted form of *puaʻa*, which means "pig."

p. 60   In the islands, "Hawaiian time" is a phrase synonymous with "late." I prefer to think of it as defining what is important.

p. 79   The phrase "outpost of solitude" comes from "The Dreamer and the Watcher," an essay by Louise Glück, published in *Singular Voices* (New York, NY: Avon, 1985), p. 81.

*

Acknowledgments

Some of these poems, a few in slightly different versions, first appeared or are forthcoming in the following publications:

Bamboo Ridge: "Calling from the Gate";
Crab Orchard Review: "Taproot" under the title "Heart Sutra #4";
CutBank: "Hawaiian Time" and "No *Pilikia*; or, Piece of Cake";
Embers: "Distance";
The Greenfield Review: "New Year's Eve" and "*Obake*";
Kestrel: "Heal-All: In Memory of Kana Nakama";
The Laurel Review: "Proteus";
New Virginia Review: "Bruises," "Immigrants," and "In My Father's House";
Pleiades: "Spheres of Influence" and "Smoke";
Ploughshares: "Aloha, 'Āina";
Puerto del Sol: "Prothalamion: Of My Brother in Los Angeles";
Tar River Poetry: "The Corsage" under the title "Remembering Your Father," "Fidelity," "Wild Horse Island," "With My Mother and Aunts in the Kitchen," "Pineapples," "Catch and Release," "Back to Back," and "The Weep Line."

Some of these poems also appeared in *Back to Back*, winner of the 1997 Harperprints Poetry Chapbook Competition.

"In the Way Back" by Debra Kang Dean, copyright © 1994 by Debra Kang Dean, from *Unsettling America* edited by Maria Mazziotti Gillan and Jennifer Gillan, is used by permission of Viking Penguin, a division of Penguin Books USA Inc.

"Back to Back" was included in the 1997 edition of *Anthology of Magazine Verse & Yearbook of American Poetry*.

Especially for their help in shaping this book, I want to thank Lee Evans, Patricia Goedicke, Peter Makuck, Greg Pape, Richard Tayson, and Thom Ward. To them and many others, like Julie Fay, Marlon Fick, Jeff Franklin, Haas Mroue, Marilyn Nelson, Luke Whisnant, and Joyce Young, I am also grateful for advice, support, and encouragement. My thanks to Steve Huff, Bob Blake, and David Caliguiri. To Colette Inez a special thanks for her seismographic reading. And, of course, to Brad and David, always.

About the Author

Debra Kang Dean was born in 1955 in Honolulu, Hawai'i. A third-generation American, she is of Korean and Okinawan ancestry. After graduating from high school, she spent one semester at the University of Hawai'i at Mānoa, then enlisted in the Air Force. She received both a BA and an MA from Eastern Washington University on the GI Bill, and in 1989 received an MFA from the University of Montana. She lives in North Carolina with her husband and two cats.

*

BOA EDITIONS, LTD.

THE A. POULIN, JR. NEW POETS OF AMERICA SERIES

Vol. 1   *Cedarhome*
          Poems by Barton Sutter
          Foreword by W.D. Snodgrass

Vol. 2   *Beast Is a Wolf with Brown Fire*
          Poems by Barry Wallenstein
          Foreword by M.L. Rosenthal

Vol. 3   *Along the Dark Shore*
          Poems by Edward Byrne
          Foreword by John Ashbery

Vol. 4   *Anchor Dragging*
          Poems by Anthony Piccione
          Foreword by Archibald MacLeish

Vol. 5   *Eggs in the Lake*
          Poems by Daniela Gioseffi
          Foreword by John Logan

Vol. 6   *Moving the House*
          Poems by Ingrid Wendt
          Foreword by William Stafford

Vol. 7   *Whomp and Moonshiver*
          Poems by Thomas Whitbread
          Foreword by Richard Wilbur

Vol. 8   *Where We Live*
          Poems by Peter Makuck
          Foreword by Louis Simpson

Vol. 9   *Rose*
          Poems by Li-Young Lee
          Foreword by Gerald Stern

Vol. 10   *Genesis*
          Poems by Emanuel di Pasquale
          Foreword by X.J. Kennedy

Vol. 11   *Borders*
          Poems by Mary Crow
          Foreword by David Ignatow

Vol. 12   *Awake*
          Poems by Dorianne Laux
          Foreword by Philip Levine

Vol. 13   *Hurricane Walk*
          Poems by Diann Blakely Shoaf
          Foreword by William Matthews

Vol. 14   *The Philosopher's Club*
           Poems by Kim Addonizio
           Foreword by Gerald Stern

Vol. 15   *Bell 8*
           Poems by Rick Lyon
           Foreword by C. K. Williams

Vol. 16   *Bruise Theory*
           Poems by Natalie Kenvin
           Foreword by Carolyn Forché

Vol. 17   *Shattering Air*
           Poems by David Biespiel
           Foreword by Stanley Plumly

Vol. 18   *The Hour Between Dog and Wolf*
           Poems by Laure-Anne Bosselaar
           Foreword by Charles Simic

Vol. 19   *News of Home*
           Poems by Debra Kang Dean
           Foreword by Colette Inez

*